T␂␂␂␂␂

OF THE

BLACK CARD

I HoPe This Book
INSPIRES You IN Life

LoVE

[signature]

THE ARTT
OF THE
BLACK CARD

THE NO BULLSH*T GUIDE
TO BUSINESS

ANTHONY RYAN SADANA

The Artt of the Black Card
The No-Bullsh*t Guide to Business

Published by Artt Press

Copyright 2019, Anthony Ryan Sadana

ISBN 978-1-7343110-0-6

Dedicated to my Father

If I've grown up to be half the man you are,
then I consider myself a success.

CONTENTS

DISCLAIMER, WAIVER AND RELEASE
READ THIS DOCUMENT CAREFULLY. IT AFFECTS YOUR LEGAL RIGHTS.

BY CHOOSING TO PURCHASE THIS BOOK AND CONTINUE reading, you and the author hereby agree as follows, and you represent and warrant that you have read and understood this disclaimer and mutual release and have voluntarily agreed to its provisions:

In exchange for the material and information contained in this book, you agree to fully and forever waive, discharge and release any and all claims, causes of action, and damages of any nature against the author, which may in any manner whatsoever arise from or relate to the contents herein. This waiver and release includes, without limitation, any claims arising from or related to the subject matter discussed herein.

The contents of this book do not constitute any warranty, promise or representation by the author.

If any provision of this agreement is held to be invalid or unenforceable, the remaining provisions shall nevertheless continue in full force and effect.

BY READING FURTHER, YOU CERTIFY THAT YOU HAVE READ THIS DISCLAIMER, WAIVER AND RELEASE, UNDERSTAND IT, AND VOLUNTARILY WAIVE AND RELEASE CERTAIN SPECIFIED LEGAL RIGHTS AS SET FORTH ABOVE.

ACKNOWLEDGMENTS

To my doctor and dear friend, Julio Garcia, who started me on this path.

To my friend, Michele Morgan, for your friendship and guidance.

To my husband, David Gravel, for supporting me through this entire process.

To my friends, Kevin Benoit and Guillaume Jobin, who constantly had my back in all my business endeavors.

To Bob Burris and Brian Rouff for your direction and advice.

To Joseph Miranda-Steele for your tireless efforts and editing on my behalf.

And to my mother, Paola Rocchi, for always being there.

PREFACE

NINETY-NINE PERCENT OF PEOPLE IN THE WORLD WOULD KILL THEMSELVES IF THEY HAD TO GO through what I've gone through to get where I am today. The stress alone should have killed me, and on many days, I wonder how it hasn't. Through many hard decisions and difficult times, I have learned a lot about business and what it takes to succeed. I've experienced so many highs and lows and rebuilt myself so many times that a vast majority of people would have given up a long time ago.

I am an entrepreneur in the truest sense of the word.

I'm not here tell you a story of how I turned a hundred dollars into a hundred million. I'm here to describe for you the realities of what it takes to make it by building your dream from the ground up. Glamor is for entertainment. What you are reading will provide you with real and tangible knowledge. This is not another 'get-rich-quick' scheme book; these are the stories of my ups and downs, and the sacrifices I've made to actualize my dreams. You will notice a disclaimer, waiver and release at the front of this book. This disclaimer is necessary because in order to offer the unfiltered truth, I must limit any possible recourse against me.

This is my journey.

I was born and raised in Montreal, Quebec. My father always pushed me to get a good education to fulfill his vision of a future for me where I worked my way up the corporate ladder. He is an entrepreneur himself, and all I can remember as a kid was his astounding work ethic and the numerous hours he spent at his office daily. I listened closely to his lessons; I'm guessing his advice was meant to guide me down a path he deemed "easier," but as they say, "The apple never falls far from the tree." I sometimes look back and wonder if my life would have been easier following the corporate ladder instead of the road less travelled. Easier possibly, but not as fulfilling.

When I was just eleven or twelve years old, my parents sent me to a boarding school called Cardigan Mountain School in Canaan, New Hampshire. That was where I got my first taste of entrepreneurship, starting me on the path to becoming the man I am today. It is an all-boys boarding school, with a militia-style education. We all wore suits and ties to our classes and disobedience was met with appropriate consequences. My classmates were some of the wealthiest kids in the United States. Among them were Jacques Cousteau's grandson, as well as an heir to the Revlon cosmetics company. I was different from them in many ways. The most obvious distinction being my father was not wealthy along the standards of the other kids in my school. He worked hard to send me to this boarding school, and he did it to give me additional tools necessary for life.

One of my earliest memories as an entrepreneur began in boarding school. They served a lot of meals I wasn't eager to eat, so I compromised with a mini-freezer filled with frozen meals. My dad helped, and every few weeks he sent me cash to restock. I bought all sorts of snacks, and in just a few short days realized the kids at school wanted some too. Putting two and two together was easy. The next day I began selling them for a hefty markup, and not only to my fellow students, but to faculty as well. We were pretty much in the middle of fucking nowhere, and I was basically the only access point for a can of Coke most nights on campus. I understood supply and demand, and my instinct for capitalization meant at the end of every school year I would have a lot more money than I started with.

That's where my entrepreneurial spirit began to take shape. This mindset has benefitted me my whole life. At the peak of my success as an adult, I have done business with many major Fortune 500 companies and celebrities alike. From one end of the world to the other, and one extreme to the next, I have worked with big-name celebrities like Kiss in Los Angeles, and brands like Pepsi as far away as Africa.

I haven't always been directly dishonest, but much like a tightrope walker, being an entrepreneur often means dealing with what is best referred to as "the gray area." It's a constant balancing act, which I will demonstrate later. Balancing requires self-control; it is not always necessary to put all your cards on the table, and it is still profoundly bold to go all in. The point of this book is to show all the risks I've taken, all my failures and successes, and inspire other people — inspire them not to give up, to remind them that tomorrow is a new day, that everything happens for a reason and when you look back at your life, it's only then you will be able to connect the dots and appreciate what you've accomplished.

Even something that looks like a failure can be the building block for your next triumph. I know this is true because I've lived it. I've been stupid, I've blown a lot of money, I've made bad deals. But because of this I've learned a lifetime of lessons and earned millions based on my hard-won knowledge. I've always gotten up one more time than I've been knocked down. I am currently in my late thirties, but I am often told I talk like someone who has had the life experience of an eighty-year-old. And on most days, I feel like it as well.

On my worst days when I've had no money and needed to bounce back, I've gotten behind my computer and worked like a dog. Where most people would sit at home, close the door, put a pillow over their head and want to die, failure has motivated me to work harder and smarter. I wake up earlier the next day and I get to work. I figure out what I have to do. Where and how I can make money. One of the biggest keys to success in any capacity is your ability to say *fuck you* to excuses and accept responsibility for every one of your actions. This includes debts. I've never screwed anyone for a dollar in my life. I've never owed anyone a dollar I haven't paid back. I live off my word. If a project or a plan doesn't work out, I throw it in the garbage, cut my losses and I move on to the next idea. People live too much in the past instead of just moving forward. You should know when to stop throwing good money after bad and move on.

You might be wondering why I decided to base the title of this book on the American Express Black Card (officially the "Centurion Card"). It's because the Black Card is a benchmark of success; it represents the pinnacle of my financial achievement and remains the standard by which I measure myself every single day. There is a shroud of mystery surrounding the Black Card. People don't know much about it, let alone how you go about getting one. (The number of cards issued each year and the qualifications for acquiring one are closely held secrets.) The public might have only heard about it in rap songs or in movies. There are no advertisements for the Amex Black Card and you can't apply for it. It's issued by invitation and only to those who have proven themselves successful at the highest financial level are invited. No one gives you an award for doing well in life. Earning a Black Card is the ultimate recognition for measuring any sort of achievement against your peers.

I was twenty-three years old when my invitation came. I remember the moment I was invited like it was yesterday. I returned home one day to find a black cardboard box sitting on the dining table. I slowly glanced at the return address, as if I didn't really want to confirm my suspicions. The sender's address I knew very well: it was that of American Express. I knew exactly what I was about to open. How this moment affected me and made me feel is impossible to describe. After I collected myself, I cut open the black cardboard box and inside sat a black wooden box with black tissue paper and a formal invitation to acquire the Centurion Card. When I called to accept, they already knew me because of my frequent interactions with the company.

"Mr. Sadana," said the voice on the other end of the line, "you are one of the youngest clients we have had work their way up to a Black Card. You are part of a very elite circle of people who have been chosen. You should be proud of your achievement."

I didn't need to be told how important this was. Being offered a Black Card told me I had done something right, and that I was being recognized for it. I had worked so hard to achieve financial freedom and it felt as though I was on top of the world in that moment. It also made me feel invincible: the card, crafted of anodized titanium, has no limit. I now could realistically buy anything I wanted, and on some days I did. Little did I realize how short-lived that feeling of power would prove to be.

I share this to illustrate that just like me, you'll experience highs and lows in your finances and in other aspects of your life. If you set a goal, don't let anything stop you from achieving it. And once you reach that goal, it does not mean your journey is through. At twenty-three, a Black Card was the culmination of my success up to that point in my life. Perhaps a master's degree is your Black Card, or opening up a small business. It doesn't matter. It's the journey that counts, and my goal in this book is to give you the tools you need to get through the bad times — then emerge stronger than ever.

In the pages that follow, you'll learn nine vital work/life principles, backed by my stories as an entrepreneur. These principles and ideas are my sincere thoughts that have helped me along my path and should motivate you along your own journey. Whether you are established or just starting out, this book will guide you through my own trials and triumphs, and give you solid, realistic advice on how to succeed and keep fighting to build your dreams as an entrepreneur.

Chapter 1

BE ON THE LOOKOUT

IF YOU SKIPPED THE PREFACE AND MOVED RIGHT ON TO THIS FIRST CHAPTER, YOU ARE DOING YOURSELF A disservice in understanding what is to follow.

No one is ever going to knock on your door and hand you a check for doing nothing. You are dependent on your own motivation to inspire yourself to do more than just sit at home and wait for tomorrow to come. In order to be a successful entrepreneur, you must see opportunity where others do not. You must be on the lookout 24/7 and always be on alert. Over time this will become a driving force of habit and will begin to work for you on a subconscious level. In this state of mind your nature will transform. It will be searching endlessly. Opportunity will strike when and where you least expect it. And when it does, be ready to move quickly and decisively.

I have built a great life for myself flipping inventory. The old adage goes: one man's trash is another man's treasure. The only thing I have changed over time is what I was pushing at that moment. I have never believed any money existed in building something from scratch. I always felt there was more money in liquidating others' failures than building something new. When you sell what someone has already mentally written off, there is a huge profit to be made. If you know how to connect distressed assets with a buyer, you have the perfect equation for building wealth. It can be done with a box of toothbrushes or an antique necklace; this rule extends itself to everything, no matter how big or small. I could flip something as little as a single lamp, or as large as a multimillion-dollar company. My flipper's arsenal of tools consists of: eBay for small items; Craigslist for large and heavy pieces; my experience and ability to auction items; and occasionally the assistance of a savvy business broker and even better lawyers. With these tools, I have been able to conquer every deal presented to me. Sometimes I would buy out the company or inventory directly and then figure out how to move it; other times I would represent the merchandise until it was sold through one of my platforms. Most of the time I would make the exact same money on owning the items or simply representing a deal, so neither really had an advantage. Yet because I built a name for myself in the liquidation industry over so many years, it was always preferable to not require capital for financial gain, and as the years went on and I built a stronger reputation, companies would turn to me for my expertise more often than for capital.

You never know who you're talking to. You never know who the person you just met is and how they could change your life. You cannot know what tomorrow is going to bring. So often it is the people you least expect who will impact your life and/or help you achieve your goals. As a life lesson, it is crucial to keep an open mind when meeting new people. This principle extends itself nicely into entrepreneurship as well. *I have learned a million times that you are who you hang out with,* and while not everyone is going to be there forever or offer the kind of growth and potential you would like, it is still imperative to *never brush off anyone you meet.* Go ahead and read those italics again, say it in your head with that emphasized voice. At the end of the day, each unique experience you have with any particular individual is going to offer an opportunity, and more often than not you will benefit from this interpersonal transaction. Each individual will serve a purpose in your personal development as an entrepreneur. Everyone's advice and personality are going to shape you into the businessperson you become.

So how do you develop the mindset of always being on the lookout? Well, practice.

Not to be a smartass (okay, maybe a little), but it's completely built into me over years of practice and habit. And it can be for you too; you just need to train yourself to always be thinking and always be looking. I could be at a party having a conversation with someone who's telling me about how they were at their Aunt Lisa's house this weekend and she inherited the biggest collection of antique coins you've ever seen, and while he's talking, I only hear this: "Blah, blah, blah… antique coins… collectible…" And I'm thinking, "Oh my God, what if she wants to sell them? What if she doesn't know *how* to sell them?"

Of course I am respectful enough to let him finish his story, but then I start digging. In order to make a deal I need to know very limited information: "Does she want to sell them? Do you know what they're worth?" With this I can determine if the deal is worth taking on. Let's say Aunt Lisa came into this collection and simply wants to get rid of it; I might make a fast offer and determine later how to offload the merchandise. It always helps to understand the market for items you're purchasing, but more often than not you get a very precise window of opportunity, and this is where learned instinct kicks in. The same instinct I am demonstrating in this book. I've made many profitable deals in exactly this way. Of course, I have lost on deals as well. Yet, this is the beauty of entrepreneurship. It is art. Each calculated risk transforms tomorrow.

My brain doesn't distinguish between small or large transactions, all it absorbs are opportunities to make a deal. It can be for something small, like a pair of sneakers on sale at Adidas, or twenty-five containers from General Electric filled with liquidated merchandise. There is money to be made at every extreme. My mind hears what is beneficial to it no matter the size of the item or potential financial gain. It's sort of like asking a dog, how do you develop a great sense of smell? Although I was born with good instincts, the finer techniques have been honed and enhanced over years of practice and habit. You must train yours to realize opportunity in the same ways that I have.

Don't forget that being on the lookout does not always mean directly searching for profitable transactions, but also seeking people with great life experience who can teach you from their own perspective and lend advice that enhances your personal development. You are who you surround yourself with. I would never be where I am today if it were not for CEOs, entrepreneurs, and likeminded individuals I befriended during my journey. Sometimes these relationships are short-lived, and many others have stood the test of time. The lesson here is that every individual is an asset, and after learning this, I was able to transform how I viewed interpersonal relationships. Their impact on my life, especially in my younger years, has shaped me for better or worse. And ultimately made me the man I am today.

A few years back, after living in Florida for a while, I found myself financially constrained. Not because of bad spending habits or living a lavish lifestyle. Florida was great to me; it is the reason I live in the United States today. I made hundreds of thousands of dollars living in Florida, but all of that money went to paying for mistakes left behind in Canada. When I felt like Florida had served its purpose, I remembered a time when I wanted to live in Las Vegas. In need of a fresh start, I decided to pack my dog, my belongings, and random accoutrements into my Mercedes. I hit the road with four thousand dollars in my pocket, clutching a dream that the West Coast was going to be a different and better market. I trusted that whatever I'd done on the East Coast was merely a stepping stone for what was soon to come. When I arrived in Las Vegas, I used the last of my savings to rent a furnished condo for the first month. I figured everything was going to work out the same way Florida had for me. If you assumed my use of the word "figured" implies it didn't work out, well, you're right. What soon followed would be one of the greatest tests of my life.

I quickly learned there is no money to be made in Vegas, at least not in my line of work. You see, Vegas is a transient city. In this context, transient means the city is constantly in flux; there is a massive movement of population in and out. There is no wholesale, there are no liquidation deals. I started to borrow money from my friend Guillaume to pay my rent, and to make my car payments; hell, occasionally to buy toilet paper and metaphorically clean up the shit I got myself into. It wasn't long before I found myself almost eighty thousand dollars in the red and had to start thinking hard to know what my next steps were going to be. I needed to recover some ground and get myself out of the rut I was in and get back on track, back in the race, as they say. And so, I gave notice on the fancy apartment where I was staying and started to transform how I saw tomorrow.

About a month before I returned the keys, I said "Fuck it, I'm going to put an ad on Craigslist to rent out the second room in my apartment." It was beautifully furnished in an upscale complex. A little Indian woman named Arti, perhaps sixty-five years old, accepted my ad and rented the room for thirty dollars a day with an additional ten dollars a day to chauffeur her to and from meetings. During this period of my life, I really had nothing else going on other than selling merchandise on eBay (which has been a constant in my life), except it wasn't enough to bring in any real, viable income. Although I'd relocated to Las Vegas, my business contacts across the U.S. were still contacting me with liquidation deals available on the market. A few years back I did some liquidation business with Macy's in Los Angeles. As fate would have it, two days prior to my tenant's departure, my L.A. contact called me with thrilling news, and got straight to the point:

"Hey Anthony, we've got a deal. Thirty-five truck-loads of furniture. We need it gone."

Although I eagerly wanted this deal, I didn't have the space it would require to warehouse thirty-five truckloads of furniture nor the capital to start renting a space and trying to sell it off piece by piece. Despite this, I printed out the information and forgot it on my dining room table. I remember it being about eighty-five pages of inventory. Macy's total cost was roughly seven hundred thousand dollars, the retail value exceeding $3.5 million. Ever on the lookout, I recognized if the space and funds were available to me, I could negotiate the lot at a steal for twenty-five thousand dollars. Please take note: a majority of the time, companies care more about the space than they do the loss. If you try and imagine a warehouse, every square foot of flooring and shelving has a relative cost to storage ratio for the merchandise on hand. It does not make sense for a corporation to hang on to inventory that is not moving. Similarly, for small business owners reading this book, there is a calculable cost of price density per square foot that is a valuable tool for profit, i.e. don't hold or buy merchandise that is worth $2 per square foot versus $3 per square foot; if you do, you've instantly barred yourself from fifty percent more profit. At any rate, Macy's (and other large corporations) would rather sell — liquidate — stagnant merchandise cheap to a liquidator and move to on to something else than store end-of-season or mixed items at a huge financial cost. To extend my point, by not liquidating certain merchandise, it actually places a larger storage burden on already-troubled storage infrastructure. In this particular instance, Macy's had furniture sitting in trucks in the loading docks. So not only were their trucks not being used to haul in new merchandise, their lot was full of inert product. I knew this could be the deal of a lifetime, as they needed me to remove this old merchandise so they could resume normal productivity. Time is money after all. The space to them was more valuable than the loss.

On the last night before she left (a mere six days later) Arti came home and asked if I'd like her to make dinner for me. I gladly accepted. I have visited India a few times and adore the cuisine. That night we had a simple meal of potatoes and rice with warm Chapati bread and while we sat at the table eating, she saw the stack of papers from Macy's.

What do you suppose Arti did for a living?

Completely unknown to me, she owned the biggest chain of furniture stores in Massachusetts. She was worth an incredible thirty million dollars and was staying at my place for thirty dollars a night, making me vegetarian food, and paying me ten dollars to drive her around. I later learned the reason she was renting the room from me was much more humbling. She wanted to demonstrate to her employees that they didn't need to stay in fancy hotels when traveling for business on her dime. The lesson to her staff was that if she can be comfortable renting something like an Airbnb, they could do the same. (She was also a bit stingy.) This should be a lesson to you as well; even when you can afford extravagance, choose only what you need. If you are making four thousand a month, you don't need a lease for eighteen hundred dollars or a car for eight hundred dollars. Anyway, Arti ended up buying the deal from me for $185,000. I quickly turned around and purchased the offer from Macy's for $25,000. She pulled out a pile of cash from her purse and left me a deposit on the spot. I knew she was not playing around and was a serious buyer. As they say, "She put her money where her mouth was."

That woman saved my life without even knowing it. The funny thing is, because I was living in a beautifully furnished condo and driving a brand-new Mercedes, she had no idea how broke I was at the time. If I had told her how badly I needed the money, she would have never bought the furniture from me. She thought I was wealthy; she was under the impression things were going smoothly from her knowledge of my being a liquidator. She figured if Macy's is dealing directly with me, I was someone to be taken seriously. I am, but the point is I needed this deal more than she knew. No deal comes without its own challenges. It's great to make a deal, but until cash is in hand and the customer has received their goods, anything can go wrong — and often will. The arrangement with Macy's was the furniture had to be gone, and it had to be gone *fast;* hence the reason I got such a steal. Not only that, but Macy's requires you to load your own trucks, and their employees are not insured to pass the door of the loading dock. Protocol has Macys' employees bringing goods to the docks; from here, my ragtag team of spontaneously hired haulers needed to load — by hand — all thirty-five trucks' worth of inventory. It was approximately twenty-eight hundred pieces of large furniture. Try to assemble an army in a city you have never been to that's capable of lifting and loading furniture onto thirty-five trucks over a four-day period. The mania was unreal! But I live for this; chaos is my tea.

I got the job done. I remember hiring the Macy's security guy's nephew and son to help out with the load. With everything loaded and shipped, she paid me the balance due as well as cutting me a check for the employees' wages. All this was possible because of a simple ad on Craigslist to rent a room and because my eyes were open for opportunity. Another factor to consider is that I did not let the fact that I was virtually broke dull my edge, I still chased the challenge and prevailed. Most people without the proper mindset and knowhow would have never been able to convert that opportunity into such a big sale. Still, knowing who you are dealing with and how to handle them is only half the battle.

You never know when lightning will strike. In early 2015 I was at a doctor's office in Beverly Hills for a procedure, and while we were talking he told me about a bunch of surplus medical equipment he had in storage. Initially he'd had plans to open his own surgical center, but after evaluating costs it was no longer a feasible project. Having already purchased all the equipment and having no use for it, it sat in storage somewhere in North Hollywood. I told him I was a liquidator, but at the time I didn't really know where I could flip it.

Three years later, I got a call out of the blue from a consultant in Mombasa, Kenya, who was putting a hospital together and needed medical equipment at heavily discounted prices. The people there had found me through a gentleman who purchased some medical items I had in an auction some years prior. By no means was I any sort of medical supplier, but my reputation through my industrial auctions found its way overseas to Mombasa. Luckily for me this would be another tight break to make a fast dollar. They told me they were in the market for hospital equipment and asked me to help them get what they needed.

"Send me a list of what you're looking for," I said.

Upon reviewing this list, I quickly realized I had no idea what any of it was, but like any good businessman, if I wanted to make money I certainly needed to learn, which is another key point to being an entrepreneur — adaptability. See, I had never really dealt in hospital equipment in my life, but in a matter of forty-eight hours, with the help of YouTube, I taught myself what I needed to know about the equipment in question. And after doing my due diligence, I knew right away who I needed to call: the doctor in Beverly Hills.

When he answered, I introduced myself and got straight to business. "You did a procedure on me three years ago. Is the surplus medical equipment we talked about still available?" Lo and behold, it was. Even three years later I was not surprised to learn he still had it. I relayed the list and tallied a deal on the items, we shook hands and I walked away with a tidy profit. The rest of the items he was unable to provide I purchased off eBay for my contact in Mombasa. I also gathered inventory from a few other medical providers looking to dump equipment no longer up to American standards, but still viable in third-world countries. In these situations, everyone is a winner. I was able to help supply medical equipment to a hospital in need; I helped the doctor recover some of the investment he made years prior; and I ended up putting my profits in the stock market and came out with even larger gains. Just by being aware and connecting the dots, I was able to close a deal and make a sale most others would not have bothered with.

I recognize the skill of always being on the lookout can appear daunting. Many young entrepreneurs are afraid to ask, are fearful of rejection, or are disillusioned in understanding every opportunity is potentially limitless. My ability to recognize opportunity has saved my ass many times and I think my entire life has been about finding those opportunities and making the most of them. I have learned so many times that opportunity comes from the oddest of situations and when you least expect it. Being hungry is never going to be enough. You need nourishment to satisfy hunger, so start small. Network. Take the minimum-wage job. Stay awake at night researching a new skill or negotiate a deal on an online marketplace. You have to want it. You have to hunt. You *must* hunt. I have always felt like my senses have been more alert during dry spells. It's as though my brain knows when we are on the hunt for the next big deal, and like a blind dog searching for food with his heightened sense of smell, my subconscious is on the prowl.

Learn to *be on the lookout* for both financial opportunity and human interaction. Make the most of possibilities that other people might walk right past. Be different, be wise, be determined.

Chapter 2

LOVE WHAT YOU HATE

IT IS OFTEN SAID IF YOU LOVE WHAT YOU DO, YOU NEVER HAVE TO WORK A DAY IN YOUR LIFE. YET HOW OFTEN ARE people really living their dream? Often enough it is not possible, so you must make do to get ahead of the curve so that one day you can escape the dreaded nine-to-five. You're not always going to love what you have to do to make money, but suck it up and realize that it could be worse. Even on your worst day, you are almost always dealing with first-world problems.

Are you having troubles with a customer, supply chain, someone not paying you what they owe or trying to screw you on a deal? Remember, you could be living in a remote village in a poor country without electricity and walking five miles each way to the closest water source. The idea is right now you are most likely in a developed country reading this book; you are not always going to love what you do or what you have to do to make money, and that's okay. What is not okay is making excuses to not work. At the end of every day, when you are watching TV on the couch or playing the hottest video game in your free time, you are avoiding responsibility.

The idea of loving what you hate and how this concept will help you transform tomorrow is learning to view everything around you as a tool. Your current job is just a tool to get where you want to be. You should love how much you hate it, because if you hate it enough you will choose to evolve beyond it. Spread your wings. Or grow a pair — of legs. Use your frustration constructively. It is a powerful transition to transform frustration to fruition. Everything can grow, even in the worst soil, if you care for it properly. At the end of the day, you're all you've got. Act like you care.

Options always exist. You could be working for someone else, but you *choose* to work for yourself. For a person with an entrepreneurial mindset, this is by far the best option, but not the only path. Sometimes you need to take a step back, get a regular job, regroup, recapitalize, and get a steady paycheck for a while. Collect yourself, then come back even stronger and more determined. Believe me, many times I have done just that. This is something I will cover later in the book.

eBay changed my life. The great thing about eBay is no matter how bad things get, you can always use their platform and sell something. When I've been at my lowest, eBay has always been there for me. I would estimate that over the years, I've done about seven to ten million dollars' worth of business on eBay, based on a half million per year of sales at least. eBay has been a very successful platform for me, and given that, you would probably think I love it. Some things about it I do. But by no means is it glamorous.

I absolutely hate having to wake up every morning and ship eBay items. I hate it to this day, and that will never change. The way my eBay has been set up in the past is in a garage or warehouse. In order to become a top-rated seller, you must ship items the same day they're ordered and offer a fast turnaround. I also must respond to customer feedback, check local auctions and opportunities for liquidation, and manage my own stock. The business itself is a job and a half. Some days I go to bed physically exhausted and mentally drained. It completely commits you to being tied to your office five, six, sometimes seven days a week and unable to travel because you are obligated to ship items within twenty-four hours of a purchase. The process of building an eBay store is exhausting, but after months of effort, I could maintain all of the integrated tasks in just a few hours a day. I love that. I also love the financial revenue I get from it. I understand that in order to get to where I need to be, I must perform the next day better than I did the last. I am constantly focused on streamlining my process. (Eventually I would be operating several businesses at once, in the same time it took to operate just the one.) The initial investment into any project is going to be costly; this is going to include massive sacrifices of time and money, but the end result is worthwhile. If you want to train your brain to think smarter, take every small task you do, analyze it heavily, and determine how it can be done faster. Efficiency is your friend in every aspect of your life. Master this and you can master anything. To summarize this point, you're not going to always love what you have to do to make money, but bite the bullet and keep things in perspective. It's a necessary evil. No whining allowed.

You don't always need a large amount of money to create something. You can accomplish big things with a minimal investment. Once I had completed the deal with Macy's, I used that money to pay off many bills owed to credit cards and friends after a very financially dry year in Las Vegas. I found myself with a clean slate, but no capital to move on to something new. I did not want to find myself in the same position I was in during my short Vegas stint, so I knew I had to start something quick.

I was now living in Los Angeles. The deal with Macy's kept me in L.A. for a few weeks and I had no reason to return to Nevada. So with my friend Kevin I got a place in West Hollywood and started to shape what would be the next major chapter in my life. I was now debt-free, and with the Los Angeles market in front of me, the opportunities were endless. One afternoon Kevin asked what it would take for me to rebuild. I said I could recover on just fifteen hundred dollars and he immediately offered to loan me the money. Of course I accepted.

I used half the money as a deposit on a small warehouse and I spent the other half on a bunch of merchandise from all around L.A. I didn't care what it was, whatever I could get for $1 and under in large quantity, I bought. Along the way, I was getting more than just inexpensive merchandise, I was starting to make a name for myself as a new liquidator in town. I was able to start establishing what would later be my biggest cycle of profit yet. I decided I was going to go big on the one thing that was there for me my whole life: eBay. After filling the shelves of my little warehouse, I started listing and listing and listing. Did I mention I was listing? Within six months that business went from doing a few hundred dollars a day to thirty to forty thousand dollars a month. I hated all the hours typing in listings, packing up merchandise, and making endless trips to the post office. Except I learned to love it. eBay ended up building me a new path to a new fortune. This new interest would soon compound into the next big avenue I would pursue.

Years prior in Montreal, I had met an auctioneer named Miki. At sixty years of age, Miki was a very successful industrial auctioneer. We had met through a retail operation I had for sale, and Miki was interested in purchasing it for his wife. We instantly connected as friends. We never ended up doing the retail deal, but we spent every weekend together and the friendship I gained was worth far more. His experience as an auctioneer rubbed off on me. I now began to see an even bigger picture with the warehouse of my eBay merchandise. Keeping in mind how companies liquidate to make room for more valuable and relevant inventory, I could see the possibility to auction off my own stock. I decided to become a licensed auctioneer on the very same platform he was licensed on. My former friend now became my competition. You can always find something to sell on eBay, but in the same way, someone or some business always has something they can't get rid of and is willing to auction off.

Just the other night, I was going through and cleaning my desk drawers and I found an old Platinum American Express Card I could have tossed in the trash. Instead, I took a minute to look on eBay and found out it would sell for $200 as a completely cancelled card. Most people would have never bothered to check eBay. That card made me money. In another instance, my car had a built-in air-freshening system with bottles that magnetize onto the car and automatically circulate a scent so the interior always smells new. My first impulse was to throw the old bottles in the garbage; instead, I put two on eBay for $150 and sold them because somebody had figured out a way to refill them and put them back into cars. To further my point, everything is worth *something* to someone. I have sold used underwear and torn books. I've seen people pay money for dirt. Actual dirt. Who does that?

The point here is you must learn to recognize opportunity where others do not. I extend this topic back to being on the lookout. If you are reading this and want to start a business out of your home, start with what you have lying in front of you, start with your grandfather who has hoarded for the last twenty years. Your neighbors are moving? See if you can get a deal on a bunch of their belongings. List your items online, whether that is eBay, Craigslist or any phone app. I used fifteen hundred dollars to create a business in six months that earned more monthly than many earn in a year. This is not because I am better than you or your neighbor. It is because when I see opportunity I pounce, and I attack it hard with vigor and excitement. The same way my neighbor's kid screams into this TV playing Call of Duty, I scream into the void, give it everything I have, and take twice as much back. And you can too. But you must always be on the lookout and be ready to love what you hate. I won't say I turn trash into treasure, but I'm open to the opportunity of turning anything into whatever I can — whether I love doing it or not.

It's not only about setting up the business itself, but how you run it; that's ninety percent of the game. Recently I was on a gambling vacation in Laughlin, Nevada, and I had one of the worst nights I've ever had. Massive losses. I won't even go into those details, but I do enjoy letting loose just a little bit. At 2 a.m. I decided to go play again and I won back everything I'd lost and then some. The next day around 1:00, I decided to call my employee to see how things were going at home with listing new inventory on eBay. No answer; I couldn't get ahold of him. Something was definitely wrong. I logged onto eBay and confirmed my suspicions: no one had shipped the items for the day. They had to go out by 5 p.m. and if they didn't,

I'd be penalized for three items and lose my top-rated status, which would cut directly into sales. I have had this happen before and it took a year to recuperate. I'd already paid for four nights at the hotel and it was just my first night there. This was necessary 'me' time, but duty calls, right? Responsibility is a bitch. I realized that my employee hadn't bothered to show up and didn't even have the courtesy to call me. At that point, the vacation took a back seat to protecting my business interests. I hopped in my car, hauled ass all the way back from Laughlin to Las Vegas — a 1.5-hour drive I did in fifty-five minutes. I shipped three items totaling thirty-five dollars and lost my other three nights at the hotel. I had no choice but to stay in Las Vegas because I was obligated to ship the next day as well and did not know if my employee would pull a no-show again.

Most people would have said, "Screw it, I'm not going to drive back for thirty-five dollars' worth of items." Many individuals I tell this story to have the same reaction when I ask how they might respond in a similar situation. This is largely due to priorities and lack of foresight. If you spent eight hundred dollars on a hotel to take a small break from a crazy life and couldn't run your business properly because your employee didn't show up, many people might write it off and have the store closed for a couple days. This is even easier to do with something as intangible as eBay. Except understanding foresight and the ramifications if I did not return to ship far outweighed my temporary comfort. Whether I liked it or not, after those four days it was right back to the chopping block; I chose myself over comfort. And you, good reader, will need to do the same during your pursuit of business. I recognized returning to ship my items realistically saved me a hundred thousand dollars or more in future sales. I drove nearly a hundred miles an hour the whole way, somehow managed to avoid a speeding ticket or worse, and got the orders shipped out. I hated it, but I did it. I can give you a thousand occasions where I had to go the extra mile (or ten) because I gave someone my word.

When I lived in L.A. and ran auctions, a customer bought a full pallet of merchandise and I made arrangements for pickup by a local trucking company. That morning, I woke up sicker than I've ever been, running a high fever, shaking, hallucinating, throwing up. Still, I had committed to being at the warehouse and making sure that the materials got picked up according to our arrangement. As the day progressed,

I grew even sicker. While I was waiting for the truck to show up at the facility, I grabbed a few dusty blankets and cardboard boxes, and slept for hours on the cold cement floor. Later, my friend Kevin confided that he thought I was going to die that weekend. Well, I somehow survived. The merchandise got picked up and delivered on time and in good shape, and I kept my promise despite long odds. I had no choice, really. That's just what entrepreneurs do. Love what you hate. Remember, if you are self-employed you are the CEO. You are the captain, and if you don't focus you will go down with your ship. You might even have employees someday, but the difference between you and an employee is an employee goes home at the end of the night. Your job is twenty-four hours a day, seven days a week, whether you like it or not. You only get paid if your product sells. In all levels of business, the CEO is often the 'be all, end all' and holds the responsibility for the success of that company. It's all part of the cost of business. I absolutely hate what I do. But I absolutely love it as well.

There were times when I had to take jobs I didn't want with companies I had no respect for, but it was a necessary discomfort to stay liquid and continue pressing forward. This is what I recommend to many young entrepreneurs I come across — especially kids in high school and college who have very little or no expenses: start working and use the money to purchase goods for reselling. Reselling as a whole is the easiest avenue for young adults to dive into entrepreneurship, whether this is an avenue with eBay and liquidated stock, or buying and selling used cars. I had a friend in high school who cooked brownies at home and sold them for three dollars apiece. That kid made thousands. Admirable.

It is easy to get sucked into a successful lifestyle and swear off the nine-to-five forever, but this is not always realistic. You will make mistakes, and you will find yourself down a deep rabbit hole, desperately clawing for a way out. Well, the answer to this is often taking a small job for small money and putting that money toward something bigger. It is easy to rebuild; I have done it dozens of times. Whether due to needing a fresh start or simply building a business parallel to an existing one. Years ago, I had a rough patch and needed to take a job at Blockbuster (remember them?) so I could ride the tide through to my next big deal. Sometimes you just need to swallow your pride and bite the bullet. I didn't want to work a minimum-wage job. I hope everyone's goal in life is to move on to bigger things. Yet minimum wage was temporary and necessary to press forward. I've been a flight attendant as well. It was incredibly enjoyable, but I still thirsted for more. I've clerked at banks and put in time at the U.S. Consulate. I've poured drinks as a bartender in clubs. I toiled away at Tri-Mack Trucking. I manned the phones for American Express at twelve dollars an hour with a Black Card in my pocket. I hated it but I learned to love it because I knew it was only temporary.

At the time I decided to apply at American Express, I was in between my gig at the U.S. Consulate and buying a UPS store. I knew it would take two months to close the deal to purchase the UPS store and I still had a mortgage due and bills to pay. I decided that if I was going to pursue a temporary paycheck, I'd go for American Express. As you've read, I knew a lot about the company and was confident they'd hire me in a heartbeat. I still remember sitting in my training class with my Black Card in my pocket that cost more than what American Express paid employees like me in a month.

At one of those orientation sessions, the trainer asked us how we would properly introduce ourselves on the phone to a customer. Everybody in the class gave an example and when it was my turn I said, "'Thank you for calling American Express, my name is Anthony.' Once their name appears on the screen, I would continue with 'Good afternoon Mr. or Mrs. Jones, how are you doing today and how may I help you?' At the end of the call I'd say, 'Mr. or Mrs. Jones, can I be of any more assistance or is there anything else I can do for you?'"

"That's it," the instructor said, "you hit the nail on the head. How do you know that?"

"I've called American Express three times a day for the past twenty years," I said, "and I know exactly what they say on the phone."

The point is I didn't want to work for American Express. I very much dislike being told what to do — most entrepreneurs share this trait — but I needed a paycheck and so I did it. I know how to harbor anger toward circumstance and manifest it properly. It drives me. Think of funny cartoons where a character is so angry steam is coming out of their ears and nose. This is me. Not to say I am eternally angry, but if I am placed in a situation that is uncomfortable, I make the absolute best of that circumstance, and the steam keeps me chugging.

Most people have gotten into relationships that go sour and they get so angry over it. They're angry about the time wasted, the energy wasted and the money wasted. I always remind them that's what they wanted at the time. No one gets into a relationship because they want to get hurt. Nobody gets married because they want to get divorced. Divorce is the result of things not going right or two people growing apart over a period of time and finding that what they wanted on their wedding day is not what they want now. But you can't look back and say, "Oh my God, I'm so upset, what a waste of those years!" You got something out of it and because of that experience, you know more about what you want and what you're willing to accept or not accept in your next prospect when you find them. It makes you a more self-aware person. People are too easily disillusioned by things. That always throws me off because at one time they loved the thing they now hate.

Every decision has consequences; you may dislike them but that's what you chose. Take responsibility, buckle down and do what you have to do to succeed long term — even when it means loving what you hate. The other day, I asked my doctor, "Is it normal I can work sixteen to eighteen hours a day without feeling tired? Honestly, if I don't work that much, I don't feel human." The essence of my personality and being is to work and be productive.

"Not everyone could," he replied. "But you have incredible energy and determination. You can do what most people won't."

I've worked a lot of twenty-four-hour days in my life, pulled plenty of all-nighters. Is it because I'm Superman? No. I've learned to love what I hate, and if you want to succeed, you have to do it too. It's a mindset and a state of being.

Chapter 3

ASSHOLE

It's okay to be an asshole sometimes. But be a *conscious* asshole. Use it as a tactic when you decide it suits your purposes. You might think it will alienate people, but just as often they will respect you for it.

Being an asshole means you're ready and willing to do whatever you have to in order to succeed in life. Let me take a moment to explain. There's a big difference between being an asshole and being a complete dick.

When you're being an asshole, it's a tactic, a conscious decision on your part, and you're fully aware of what you're doing. You're not trying to make friends; you're playing hardball and you're using every tool you have to leverage the best possible deal for yourself.

On the other hand, a dick is not self-aware; they're usually acting out of fear or anger rather than consciously trying to achieve a goal and they're frequently a victim of their own behavior. Assholes get the best possible terms in a transaction; dicks piss everyone off and more often than not blow up deals that are there for the taking. To be a successful entrepreneur, there are times you need to be an asshole. But you never want to be a dick.

When I look back on when I first started my business career, I have to admit I was sometimes more sheepish and a little more malleable than I am today. Now I really know what I want, I know where I'm going and I'm more than ready to do what it takes to get there. I truly believe that in business only the strong will survive, and if you aren't willing to pull out all the stops to win, believe me, somebody else is.

My father is a very successful businessman in his own right, so very early on in my life he would impart wisdom to me. On one occasion he wanted to teach me a basic principle of the stock market. He said that you're never going to buy a stock at its lowest price and you're never going to sell it at its highest. This is a very easy concept to understand, and reading this you might think *well duh, that's pretty obvious*. The lesson here has two applications. One being that when buying and selling you will very rarely receive the lowest possible price. Take what you get and make it work. The flip side is a little more philosophical, dealing with the general comfort I get while buying and selling a stock or merchandise. I don't regret when I sell a stock for $7.50 and then it goes to $9.00 because without a crystal ball I have no way of knowing what's going to happen and neither does anyone else. You have to do the best with what you know and be happy with a profit. It is too easy as a business owner to obsess over perfect maximization; often times this overthinking can cost you money, and more importantly, your time. If something is not selling and you've made your effort, either discount it or liquidate. Keep the revolving door moving. No matter what comes after that, you have to move on. Deciding to take the risk is sometimes the hardest part; after that you have to stand behind your decision. As I stated before, find confidence in your decision-making. Learn to trust your intuition. You are always acting on what you know and what you wanted at the time.

The same philosophy applies to gambling. I've lost five thousand dollars in one session and then someone plops down next to me and wins five thousand on the first spin. I can tell you right now a ton of people would react violently to this. Maybe not externally, but five thousand dollars is a lot of money to lose. You might not be someone who would ever set foot in a casino to risk that much money, but try and imagine a scenario where you would lose that kind of money. Perhaps you have an antique watch you do not know the value of and decide to pawn it or sell it online. You've placed the value at five thousand dollars and someone buys it. You're thrilled! Except the next day this person sells the watch for fifteen thousand dollars. Theoretically you just missed out on ten thousand dollars. Perhaps you didn't lose any money outright like with gambling, but this realization is going to keep a lot of people awake at night. The purpose of this scenario is to ask you how you might react to losing a great sum of money in one fell swoop. Do you gather yourself back into a shell?

Do you simply create restrictions so it never happens again? Or do you reprioritize and devise a method of winning it back? I know many people want to do the latter, but you must really understand who you are in order to be successful. When you reprioritize to win it back, sometimes you need to be the asshole in business. The asshole accepts that these are things that are not in his or her control and cannot get angry about them. There is no sense in it. He controls the decisions he makes; this includes any emotional response. Only he controls the choices he makes. And that applies to how he conducts himself in a transaction. Sometimes you want to be the good guy and sometimes the way to get what you want is by being an asshole. The decision is always yours. You have to look out for number one, keep your eyes on the prize, and occasionally that means you have to be ruthless. It's not always easy and it hurts sometimes, but that can be the price of winning.

Let's say you had a bag of Rold Gold Pretzels and I came up to you and said, "I'd like to buy that bag from you for five thousand dollars." Your first thought would probably be that I'm some kind of nutcase. But if I went on to say, "The bag says 'gold' on it, and I'm pretty sure there's gold inside." If I then pulled out five grand in cash, you'd have a decision to make. You could take the money or you could say, "Anthony, the bag's not filled with gold. That's the name of the pretzels." That would be true — but it also means you'd be passing up the opportunity to make a quick five thousand dollars off somebody who wasn't thinking clearly or hadn't done their due diligence.

Many will respond negatively to this example. They will scream that it is immoral or a personal defect in kindness to let someone purchase something with zero value for an obscene amount of money. That is true from an external point of view. But was the seller dishonest? People will pay money for whatever they feel has value. If someone bought a bag of pretzels for five thousand dollars, they made a conscious decision to do so. The same lesson I am teaching in this book is to take ownership of your decisions. As an entrepreneur you must expect and trust that anyone approaching a transaction has also done their due diligence; it is not your responsibility to inform them beyond their preparedness. Above all else, the last time you made a mistake, you learned from it, right? It is the natural course of business to win and lose, you just happened to be on the winning side. Remember, you didn't hide anything. You didn't tell me there was gold inside. I came up with the idea myself; all you did was not say anything to stop me from closing the deal. I've been in that kind of grey area many times. I've had really hard decisions to make along the way and often the only way to justify them was that it came down to me or them. And in the case of me or them, only the strongest will survive. Make sure you approach every deal after doing your due diligence. Yes, I said earlier you often must make a deal on the fly, and there is great risk in a lot of transactions. Own the consequences. Be better next time.

For a while, I owned a giant liquidation retail warehouse in Montreal. It was the first time I opened up a liquidation outlet on this scale. Prior to the store, I was always negotiating deals without ever having to touch them, meaning I was buying and selling the deal without having to warehouse it in any way, or using my large garages for temporary needs between transactions. I wanted to try having a professional retail space to make a stable revenue source, so when the deal came up to get into this space, I took it. My warehouse consisted of thirty thousand square feet with twenty-five-foot ceilings. This building had such scale to it, absolutely massive. It had rows from front to back and you could look down the aisles to what seemed like a half a mile of clothing. You could find Columbia coats for ten dollars. Everything was two, three, five or ten dollars. People would come in who were exporting to third-world countries and buy in bulk, three hundred or four hundred items at a time. I spent thirty-five thousand dollars on my merchandise and was basically selling off the stock from that original purchase.

I had an African-American customer, a banker, who regularly came in looking for merchandise to export to Africa as a side job. He would buy three to four thousand dollars' worth of stuff at a shot, and over time I realized he had a lot of money but not a lot of business sense, at least in liquidation. My brand-new Porsche sitting in front was often a conversation-starter with customers. If I remember correctly, it was indeed my car that got him dealing with me in the first place. In an area of town that was not the best, my car stood out. I knew my customer base and I was not doing high-end retail. One time he came in and I said, "What if I sold you everything in the store?" At first, he just laughed me off, but the next time he came in he told me he'd been thinking about it — if we could make a good deal.

We started playing around with prices.

"How about one hundred thousand dollars?" I opened.

"Eighty-five thousand sounds better to me," he countered.

And that's when I realized, I was about to make a killing.

Even this number was great for me, because I knew the total value of my merchandise was five thousand dollars, maybe eight thousand on a good day. I had already raked the stock and sold everything of significant value. There was nothing but trash left. At this point, I could have told him he was vastly overpaying, but I knew it was time to be an asshole. He saw my two-hundred-thousand-dollar Porsche parked outside and assumed I'd bought it with my profits from the store. He didn't do any research; he didn't ask about my revenue. It wasn't my job to do his due diligence for him. Let the buyer beware. When you are making transactions of that caliber and at that level, it is not my responsibility to give you all the information you need. You should know what information is needed in order to make a knowledgeable purchase. You will receive what you ask for, and sometimes mistakes will become valuable lessons later in life. These principles apply in nearly all facets of a transaction, and at any level.

I stuck out my hand and sold it all to him for eighty-five thousand dollars. I couldn't believe it when the check cleared. I gave him the keys and four weeks later he closed up shop. Exactly four weeks. He didn't make it his first month. He didn't even generate enough money to pay the first month's rent. I could have told him the merchandise was only worth five thousand dollars, but it wasn't my problem. He had simply made assumptions — with no assistance from me — that weren't accurate.

When I first spent time in Vegas, I met a man named Ken Shoftstall who taught me the biggest business lesson of my life. He had an idea to build longboards from scratch and retail them locally. I was stupid. I was young. I remember going out to dinner with Ken and his wife to discuss how the business would work. They looked like they came out of a trailer park and they didn't offer to pay for dinner. That should have tipped me off — they were looking for somebody to invest in their business. I had a bit of money from the sale of a company I owned in Canada, and not recognizing the trouble signs — or doing my homework — we decided to open up Kiwi Longboards In Las Vegas, I took out a lease in a prime location on Spring Mountain Road — two years at fifty-five hundred dollars a month. I paid for everything. I took my Black Card to Home Depot and spent ten thousand dollars on woodworking equipment and everything we needed. Did I mention I was stupid? And young? I was still traveling to tend to my other businesses, but I'd fly into Vegas and I was happy to have a desk, go to lunches and have an investment in the United States. It took me two months to realize I was being robbed blind, buying more stuff than I was seeing money coming in. And nothing was being deposited in the bank.

Ken took me for the biggest ride of my life.

He sold a lot of longboards, pocketed the money and bamboozled me out of every penny I invested in that place. I went to India on a two-week vacation and while I was gone, he sold off our stock and wrote himself fraudulent checks for whatever was in the bank account. When I returned, I went back to the place and gathered whatever I could that was left, which wasn't much. I packed it into boxes, sent it by UPS to Canada to try to sell it there and recoup some of my losses. But

I was still on the hook for the two-year lease with a company that wasn't about to let me out of it. I tried going to the Nevada police. They didn't care. They went through the motions of an investigation that led nowhere. I figure I lost about a hundred thousand dollars in that deal, but what that money gave me was worth far more than anything else I could have purchased with it. It taught me lessons I would have never learned any other way. One I learned very quickly was to stay away from partnerships; they don't usually work, at least not for me. I am an independent thinker, and according to me, only one opinion counts and that is mine. Second, an absentee landlord is a great way to set yourself up for failure. I was so busy with projects in Canada, I was asking to lose my shirt. Third and most important, don't trust anyone; if someone wants your trust, they need to earn it little by little.

Can I say Ken took advantage of me? Yes. But only because I let him. He was an asshole who saw a guy with too much money and not enough brains (at least at the time) and made his move. Okay, he was a bit of a dick too, but you get the point. And in an unexpected way, he did me a huge favor: he made me into the ruthless asshole I am today. I don't lend money.

I don't care about your hard luck story. I don't care if bad breaks have forced you to sell your merchandise or business to me at pennies on the dollar. It's not my problem.

The bottom line is, it's up to you. It's up to every person in their business to decide if they're a charity or if they're out to make money. If you're out to make money, there is nothing illegal about overcharging for a service or a product. That's how the free market works and it's up to the buyer to do his or her homework and not overpay. Donald Trump is an asshole. He's also a self-proclaimed billionaire. Bill Gates is an asshole — and one of the wealthiest men on the planet. Steve Jobs was an asshole. You can be a polite asshole with class, but it's either that or be the victim.

Chapter 4

CHANGE HAPPENS

RECENTLY I WAS VISITING A BOUTIQUE HOTEL IN MIAMI WHEN A PLATE IN A GIFT SHOP CAUGHT MY EYE. IT read: "Sometimes on the way to a dream, you get lost and find a better one." I bought that plate and I look at it every day. Think about the lesson found in those few words.

If you are fixed on one idea or approach and not ready to move with the flow of change, your path to success will be difficult. For an entrepreneur, it's vital to have options — plan A, B, even C through Z if necessary. As the old boxing wisdom goes: to avoid being knocked out, you have to learn to roll with the punches. You might think you're going in one direction and by the time you reach your destination, you discover you've actually made three U-turns and ended up in a totally different place than you thought you were heading. The thing is, this is not only inevitable — it's desirable. You can't predict everything, and the smart businessperson is constantly adapting his or her goals and strategies based on the changing landscape. Change is inevitable and if you aren't ready to use that to your advantage, you're going to be left in the dust. Use the skills I teach about being on the lookout to aid you in managing change.

There have been countless times when I've had customers come in to pay for and pick up a single item from an auction I had, and I went to the front and started a conversation with them just to see what other opportunities for business might exist. Maybe they purchased the item from my auction to resell online, meaning I could pivot the conversation to other "crap" I have lying around and make an additional sale. I could potentially sell them a large lot of items to free up more shelving. Or in other circumstances, the customer would be buying something for their own business and would start to inquire as to junk they might wish to get rid of, and now acquire some new items for my next auction. They came in for one thing, but because I took the time to talk to them, they got something else. A few years back, I made a huge play in the stock market and in a very short period of time took a major hit and lost a lot of money. If that happened to most people, they would pull back, cut their losses and wait until they built their bankroll back up — a process that could take years. Instead, I decided to roll with it and said to myself, "All right, this wasn't what I originally planned and I didn't expect to be here now, but I *am* here, so what am I going to do to get past it?"

I decided to sell everything off, something I'd never planned. Any stockbroker would tell you not to do that; they'd advise you to hold on to the stocks until they turned around. But that wasn't good enough for me. My financial needs require that I have capital coming in monthly and I decided I had no choice but to sell it all, take the loss and use whatever money I had left to start reinvesting so I could rebuild as fast as possible. Did I ever think I was going to do that? No, this was not the path I set out on when I initially invested in that stock, but I realized that things change. I have one of two choices to make: change and go with the flow or sit back and cry every night. Instead of weeks of sleepless nights and unhappiness, I decided to go with something different, realize that shit happens, and make better use of that money elsewhere.

Be adaptable, be ready to think on the fly. Be willing to take a loss now to come out ahead later. Have the guts to make a course correction and salvage that loss into some sort of profit.

For most of my life, I've operated by buying and selling bankrupt retail operations but when I sold my last store in Boca Raton, Florida, I realized the retail game was dead. If I wanted to continue to be successful I had to modify my business philosophy and strategy. Here's how that insight occurred: as I mentioned before, I was born and raised in Canada, and just prior to moving to the United States at the age of thirty-one, I had accumulated three houses, two apartment buildings with twenty-four units total, drove a Porsche, had a nice truck and had made a good life for myself. I was also $2.5 million in debt on my real estate holdings. The bill for my Black Card was

$125,000 *for a single month* and I was borrowing from Peter to pay Paul just to keep my lifestyle going and get the mortgages paid. I remember looking at the card statement and wondering how the hell I allowed this to happen. How did it get so big, so fast, that I was about to lose it all?

One afternoon my auctioneer friend, Miki, called.

"Anthony," he said, "bad news. My wife is leaving me. I'm at my house in Miami. Is there any chance you can come down for a few days so I don't have to be alone?"

Like any good friend, I dropped everything and jumped on the next flight out. He had a beautiful condo in Aventura, a suburb of Miami, and we spent a couple of days catching up. I was always on the lookout for businesses or inventory to flip, and as it was my first time in Florida, I decided to check out Craigslist to see if anything looked interesting. I found a high-end women's clothing retail operation in Boca Raton that was looking to get rid of its merchandise for fifty thousand dollars. I decided to go take a look; little did I know my American adventure was about to commence.

"I want out of the business," the owner told me. "I've already invested one million dollars in this place. If you've got fifty grand, you can have all the clothing."

"What about selling me the business?" I asked. "You've got a nice retail location; I can liquidate out of here."

He told me he had a lease and that he was only interested in moving the clothes. I investigated his operation and determined why he wasn't making money.

"Let me take over the whole operation," I proposed. "Nothing up front, but I'll give you a fifty-fifty split. You just come in to pick up your money once a week. I'm in charge of running the store, sales, the whole operation." He agreed and we had a deal.

I put my ideas into action, which included slashing prices to levels the buying public would consider ridiculous but not completely insane. Instead of a T-shirt selling for twenty dollars in a regular store, he had priced it for $275. I decided it should sell for one hundred dollars. This was Boca Raton, after all, in a luxury plaza, so customers expected over-the-top pricing. But they still needed to feel like they got a deal. And it worked.

The first day using my new concepts, I pocketed five thousand dollars in sales — where he'd been lucky to do two to three hundred dollars a day. I paid him his fifty percent every week. After three weeks, I decided to ask him again, "What will it take for me to buy you out?"

By this point, the guy just wanted to cut his losses. "Ten thousand dollars cash and it's all yours." It was a steal, but as I was still $2.5 million in debt, coming up with even ten thousand was tricky. I had nothing liquid, no savings, I didn't even have any cards left that I could use for cash advances. The only choice I had was to adapt to the change in my situation. I called in every favor I could and came up with the money.

Throughout this process, I was receiving call after call every day from collection companies in Canada. I had left to spend time with Miki, but I was also escaping the financial troubles that had been piling up at home. I was working 24/7 just to keep my head above water. The only thing that kept the bank from repossessing my Porsche (I was three payments behind) was the headache of crossing borders to get it. Even though I had the store performing as well as it possibly could, I was still making no progress on getting a handle on my mountain of looming debt. So I called my successful father seeking the counsel of the one person in the world I most wanted to be proud of me.

I told him I was going to declare bankruptcy in Canada, I had no plans at the time to return home and seemed to be doing very well in Miami. I was tired of seeing all the money I was making in the United States go back to Canada just to pay off debts for a life I cared little about. As a responsible individual, I would have never filed for bankruptcy. I guess I just wanted to hear his approval.

"Anthony," he said, "it's just money. You can rebuild. If that's what you have to do, that's what you have to do."

What would you do in my situation? I didn't like the idea; in fact, I hated it because my name and reputation mean everything to me. When I say I'm going to do something, I do it. If I owe you a dollar, and you say you need it in cash, I will drive three hours and spend $150 in gas if that's what it takes to make good. But I had to get rid of my debt. As I was entertaining the idea of bankruptcy, I got a call from my real estate broker informing me that someone finally wanted to buy one of my buildings in Montreal for $1.1 million, a deal that would put $350,000 in my pocket. Forty-eight hours later, I received an offer on my home for $795,000. A day later, I accepted a cash offer for $325,000 on another lakeside property I had been sitting on for years. I now was able to cover nearly $1.5 million of my debt. Once again, it was time to change the way I was seeing and doing things.

I threw the bankruptcy mindset out the door and started to pay off my debts one by one. I continued to work the store night and day, but I knew ultimately that I couldn't make it survive; there simply wasn't enough inventory, and I didn't have the knowledge necessary to succeed in high-end women's retail. I was making good money, but the gentleman from whom I purchased the business was producing the goods overseas, designing every piece himself. I was not about to start producing and manufacturing clothing. I specialized in dismantling and selling off, not creating or designing, let alone both at once.

A customer came into the shop and expressed an interest in owning her own retail store. She told me she was sitting on some money her mother had left her, so I knew she was a serious potential buyer. I shined the store in the best possible light and sold the whole thing for $375,000 — netting me $365,000. I took a portion of the sale in cash and for the balance of sale I took a lien on the home her mother had left her in New York. When she ultimately defaulted and went bankrupt, I moved in to take the house I had been given the lien on. With a very personal connection to her deceased mothers' property, she very quickly came up with the balance of cash she owed. I learned then there is a lot of power in offering someone a balance of sale. Sometimes you're better off marking up your price and offering a balance of sale as a way to get a deal done.

Once I sold that last store, for me the retail game was dead. Things had changed and I had to completely alter what I was doing. Up to that point, I was making a lot of money on buying and selling bankrupt retail stores. Except it was getting harder to find buyers for retail. Additionally, keeping the stores afloat during the process of finding a buyer was getting exceedingly difficult, which means rather than flipping stores in a month, I was holding onto losing stores for six or seven months and those costs were killing my overall profit. I had to deal with this new market reality and figure out how I was going to move forward while respecting what I knew about buying and selling.

That's when I decided to flip the script and began providing merchandise for resellers like myself. This would help satisfy resellers who struggled to find merchandise. This new project still involved me going into mom and pop shops, or the bigger companies going bankrupt. Instead of saying, "I'm going to take the whole thing, I'm going to take the lease over," I was declaring: "I'll cut you a check for everything in here, I'll pull up a truck tomorrow, empty the place and take it back to my warehouse." Rather than beating my head against the same wall, I pivoted and found a new way to make money.

I started to realize there were a lot of eBay and Amazon sellers out there who didn't have access to merchandise. I was already buying retail operations for my own eBay stores, why not get rid of the junk I didn't need and was not going to sell to other eBayers who didn't know how to gain access to inventory. That's how I evolved into an amalgamation of both: a retailer online, a wholesaler to others. Along the way, people started asking me about how eBay works, how did my eBay operation get so big? One day I asked myself, "Why am I giving away my knowledge for free? I've been doing it for so long, why don't I start consulting?" So I did. I became a consultant and it's grown to the point where I now consult for many different companies as well as for online business. I've really rolled with the changes and naturally fell into what I do today.

There's an old saying that an animal who only eats the fruit from one tree is destined for extinction. Don't let that be you. Be ready for change, take advantage of it, and remember that when things are good (or bad) it won't last forever. Change is your ally. Make the most of it.

Chapter 5

KEEP TRANSFORMING TOMORROW

YOU CAN ALWAYS IMPROVE. YOU CAN ALWAYS DO BETTER. TRANSFORMING YOURSELF WILL TRANSFORM your situation — but it all starts with you. Each transaction, every mistake and every accomplishment should bring about change in how you transact business and handle your life moving forward. No one ever stayed in the same place and achieved success without a willingness to compromise, change and self-educate.

Keep reaching for better. If today sucked, go to bed knowing that tomorrow is still in your hands.

You have to learn from today and then transform what you do tomorrow based on your new insight. Every transaction I've ever made — whether it's for five dollars, fifty thousand dollars or five hundred thousand dollars — I've learned something from. I have taken each lesson and changed how I executed my next deal. It can be something as simple as examining every return I get from my online sales and using my research to cut down on returned items or giving better item descriptions.

Indi Chic — the women's retail clothing boutique in Boca Raton, Florida — provides an excellent example. When I first contacted the owner, I was really nothing more than a liquidator, while he was a prominent, well-established businessman in the wholesaling and production of clothing. Many businesses that go bankrupt were often started as hobbies and with little business experience; they never take off. This was the case with Indi Chic. He was tired of pumping money into his wife's "hobby" and its demise was inevitable. As I've shared, I outlined the problems with the store and told him that if he would have followed my recommendations, he would have been back on track and be able to liquidate his inventory for a lot more than what he was trying to sell it to me for.

We've all heard Einstein's principle that the truest definition of insanity is doing the same thing over and over again and expecting different results; I'm always stunned by how many people in business make this mistake. This man, for all his experience, was unwilling to change how he did business. He believed his ideas were the best and he kept pumping good money after bad. He learned nothing from startup to the point where he found himself two years later with a bankrupt store. As you read previously, I ended up buying that business and flipping it for a huge profit after implementing the exact changes he should have made.

We can always learn from everything we do. However, the sad truth is that most people don't want to learn. Most think they have the answer to everything, and that lack of flexibility and unwillingness to learn and grow is the reason the majority of businesses fail.

Many of you reading will remember when Kodak was one of the biggest, most successful brands in the world, a blue-chip corporation right up there with Coca-Cola and Ford Motors. When the digital revolution happened, Kodak could have easily pivoted and become the leading seller of digital cameras and printers in the world. Instead, they insisted that people would continue to use film. Where is Kodak today? A shadow of what it once was.

There is no shortage of examples of businesses who dug in and refused to change. How about Borders? Tower Records? Blockbuster Video?

I used to work for Blockbuster when money was tight, at just about the time Netflix began mailing out DVDs and then morphed into a streaming service. The leaders of Blockbuster Video had access to the same data and market trends, but they decided to stay the course because they had convinced themselves people would always prefer coming into a brick and mortar store to rent videos. Charging people late fees was an enormous profit center for them; it wasn't fathomable to risk losing this revenue. This had worked in the past and it made Blockbuster a household name in America, so why wouldn't it work in the future? It was that kind of thinking that got them into trouble.

Because Blockbuster refused to transform, it went bankrupt in 2010. At the time of this writing, Netflix is valued at $150 billion, more than the Walt Disney

Company. This is staggering when you stop to think about it. Even when Netflix was making a killing streaming third-party films and videos, it continued to evolve by opening a division to produce its own programming. They learned quickly that content is king. The time to innovate is not when you're in trouble, but when things are going well. That's how you stay out of trouble and keep ahead of market trends.

Coca-Cola went from making colored sugar water to buying up companies producing all kinds of beverages, from bottled water and fruit juices to sports drinks and teas. Why compete when you can buy out your rivals? Netflix and Coke understand how to keep transforming tomorrow, while Kodak and Blockbuster were fatally committed to the status quo.

The unwillingness to be moved in any way or transform how you operate dooms you for failure. Never stop asking the question: "Is it possible I could be doing business better than I'm doing it now?" Always seek methods for evolution. Just because Uncle Joe made one hundred thousand dollars a year in the ice cream business and left the business to you when he died, it doesn't mean you should continue doing it the same way. Bringing change, development, new ideas and your own life experience will bring new opportunities and new ways of making money.

You should be ready to cut your losses. Sometimes you have to know when enough is enough and move on to something else. Don't settle.

Chapter 6

Con Me If You Can

THERE IS A VERY FINE LINE BETWEEN BEING A GOOD SALESPERSON AND BEING A CON ARTIST. I'VE NOTICED that the best sales professionals, like the best con artists, make you yearn to close the deal. It's very much like fishing. All they have to do is set the hook and their work is done. A key tactic for salesmanship is making a customer believe the idea to purchase is their own. I have always felt that I was a little faster than most, and never felt vulnerable to others' tactics. That being said, I have found myself, on more than one occasion in my life, on the bad end of a deal. I usually ended up wondering if I was scammed or simply invested too quickly because I was not doing my due diligence. In retrospect, I recognize losing money always benefitted me in one way: it educated me and I learned a valuable lesson on how to be a stronger businessman. I have learned more from losing money than by making money. You have to lose to win, and that's why it's so important to start building something before you're ready. No risk, no reward. No risk, no experience. You don't want to be forty years old and just learning the ins and outs of how the business world works. It will be much harder at forty to recoup from losses and bad experiences than it would be if you started at a younger age. Start building before you're ready.

It's always important to realize that no matter how much you know, you are always capable of being conned. A few years ago, when I was living in Los Angeles, I was doing a lot of consulting for different businesses. I'd gone out to Palm Springs and rented a house for a much-needed desert getaway when a gentleman named James and his wife Elizabeth, who were referred to me, rang and said he was selling perfumes and other products on Amazon and needed help. Their business was small and they wanted advice on a path for steady financial growth.

"Look," I said. "I'm in Palm Springs, I'll be back in a month, we can meet in person when I return."

They did not seem too interested in waiting, and countered: "No, we need to meet you right away."

I responded, "Okay. Just so we're clear, it's a thousand dollars to sit down with me and you're buying lunch."

They immediately agreed. Two days later, I was sitting across the table from James at an Applebee's in Palm Springs, check in hand. We talked, I told him about my experience and what I could do for them. James must have liked what he heard because he hired me on the spot at $250 an hour.

"The first thing we need is more merchandise," James said.

"Not a problem," I replied. "I have plenty of connections for whatever you're looking for." They didn't seem to care what the merchandise was, just that they could resell it for a profit. They started buying up limited lots for one thousand, two thousand, three thousand dollars, whatever they could get their hands on locally. I found them a deal in Montreal for twelve thousand pieces of Tommy Hilfiger bathroom accessories at six dollars apiece, for a grand total of seventy-two thousand dollars. After viewing the pictures and reviewing markup, they decided it was a great deal for them, but wanted to inspect the goods prior to finalizing payment. James came to Montreal without his wife and I also flew in. He stayed in a hotel my father owned so it cost him nothing, and I spent a few days playing tour guide.

They'd deposited ten thousand dollars in my bank account prior to traveling because I made it clear I wasn't going to fly up to Canada if I didn't have a deposit in hand. The understanding was that James was supposed to bring the balance in cash.

Once we were there, he said, "I don't have enough money for the entire twelve thousand pieces," which really pissed me off. But here we were in Montreal, far away from L.A., and I had no choice at this point but to make a deal for what I could get.

"Okay," I said. "Then take half now and take half in thirty days."

"That's fine," he said.

They took eight thousand pieces right away against the ten thousand dollars they'd already deposited. They gave me another ten thousand dollars in cash and then split thirty thousand dollars between three credit cards. They then paid the four-thousand-dollar transportation charge on another credit card. A few months after returning to Los Angeles, they realized they had bitten off more than they could chew. They were not capable of handling that much merchandise. They were a couple working alone with all this Hilfiger stuff crammed into every empty space of their little house. They asked me if I could store some of it in my warehouse. I allowed them to store twenty-five hundred pieces while they got things sorted out.

The day after I agreed, this prick and his wife called their credit card companies and told them I'd accepted a return on the merchandise. They claimed they'd returned it all and I didn't provide the refund and therefore wanted the thirty-thousand-dollar balance on their credit cards removed. I was fucked because they were American Express cards and Amex always rules in the customer's favor, no matter what. With no other recourse, I tried chasing them through the Nevada court system, but they wormed their way out of that by claiming jurisdiction rights, saying they couldn't be sued in Nevada. As of this writing, I'm suing them in California and they're trying to pull the same thing, but I'm hoping the judge is going to say, "Hey, wait a minute, you already claimed in Nevada you wanted to be sued in California. Which is it? Choose one and get it over with." We'll have to see how it all works out.

Remember Arti, who I did the Macy's furniture deal with? She taught me an expensive lesson as well in the end. Our arrangement was always that I would provide her with merchandise and then bill her. On a subsequent deal, we stuck to the same plan. She gave me her American Express information and told me to charge her the $125,000 she owed the following Monday. When I contacted American Express Monday morning, I learned she'd canceled the card. When I tried repeatedly to reach her and find out what had happened, it quickly became clear that she had taken advantage of me. Fortunately, it was our third deal together and I'd made so much money I could afford the loss. Still, it hurt and I chased her for a few years in court and ended up getting paid, but the lesson came through loud and clear. One large transformation I made in how I do business due to these two transactions: I no longer take credit cards for anything over five hundred dollars. Period. Anything bigger has to be cash, check, or wired into my accounts.

I say, "Con me if you can," because that might have been easier to do once upon a time, but experiences like I've had with these folks have completely changed how I do business now. They weren't the only ones I allowed to take advantage of me. If you're not careful, you can get conned by the people you trust the most. You actually might be the most vulnerable to them.

Most of us have a close friend we see as family. Adrian was that friend for me. Growing up, and well into my adult life, he filled the role of my brother. We used to sit in the driveway and talk for hours about nothing and everything. When he was in trouble, I'd get him out. When I was in trouble, he'd have my back. He was the gayest guy you've ever seen, but the funny thing was, he was one hundred percent straight. He'd walk into a bar with an open shirt showing his muscles, Versace chains, big glasses — women would stampede to him. No one could believe he was straight and I was the gay one.

When I first came out to Adrian, he was so cool about it that he took me to my first gay bar; I can still remember the smell of the bar and that night like it was yesterday. When my parents didn't want me to become a flight attendant, you know who stayed up until 3 a.m. helping me get ready for my tests? Adrian. The day I told my father I was gay and he decided that was the perfect time to temporarily cut me off, you know who fed and sheltered me for free? Adrian. I can look in my house now and see many relics lying around that were gifts from him and his family. He was my brother through and through.

As much as he had going for him, as we grew up, he didn't really do much with his life.

"What's going on with you?" I asked. "You went to school to be a hairdresser, how come you're just hanging out and not working?"

It turns out he'd tried, but had gotten fired from two places. "I just can't work for anyone," he said.

After thinking about it for a minute I said, "I'm going to do you a big favor. I'm going to help you open your own barber shop. I'll look around for someone with an existing shop who's going under. I'll buy their shop and you can turn it into whatever you want."

That simple offer turned into a major headache, which should have been my first warning sign. He went from having nothing to a guy with all sorts of demands and requirements. He expected the shop to be in a prime location, in the right neighborhood, and he wanted it to be something he started from scratch — not taking over somebody else's business. Suddenly I went from an expected budget of ten to fifteen thousand dollars to take someone's failing business off their hands, to investing sixty-thousand-plus for a startup.

I finally found a location in Central Montreal that met all his demands and helped him sign the lease and close the deal. He had all sorts of big ideas about how this shop was going to be, all the features it was going to have.

"Adrian," I said, "it's okay to have big ideas, but sometimes you can do it on a tight budget."

Well, he didn't want to do it on a tight budget. Everything had to be top of the line. We began to argue about everything and our lifelong friendship deteriorated very quickly. My brother had become my business partner, and for the next two months I dumped every penny I had into building that barber shop — and then some. I borrowed from friends, I ran up my credit cards, all to create what became the very successful Scotch and Scissors. The two he owns are known as the preeminent barber shops in Canada. He caters to wealthy businesspeople who enjoy a premium scotch while getting their hair cut. So that's where the happy ending comes, right? Not exactly.

About two months after the first shop opened, I went to Adrian and was honest with him. "I'm not a millionaire," I confessed. "What I did, I did from my heart, but I need you to start paying me some of my money back. Let's start with one hundred dollars a week."

To date, I've gotten back somewhere in the neighborhood of fifteen hundred dollars. He claimed he was owed money from when we were teenagers, for petty things like favors not traded or lunches purchased. And the excuses never stopped. I never saw it coming because I wasn't the person then that I am today, and even if I was, I would probably do it again. There is something beguiling about doing business with friends. You ignore logic. I understand many of you reading this have had conversations with close family and confidants on opening up a store, or building a project together, believing it's your big break because of your overall compatibility. But people change when expectations are involved. People change when money can be made and lost. The prevailing reason for divorce in the world has to do with issues related to money. People don't get into a marriage because they think they are going to get divorced. This same principle applies to business; it is a consequence of being human. Think twice before setting up a joint venture and make sure you protect yourself in the process. This is why putting things in writing is a very good idea; this was my mistake with Adrian. I didn't put anything in writing because I trusted him too much. When ideas and promises are written down and contracted, nothing can be convoluted or misunderstood later. You cannot go back and say you didn't know something or were confused with the process.

Let me expand on Adrian a little more. When we began the project, we had a verbal agreement I would be a fifty percent partner due to my having the available funds and ability to make the dream happen. As the transaction matured, it devolved from a partnership into, "I'll just pay you back what you're owed." I eventually wrote off our friendship and his debt altogether. I accepted it as life experience.

I didn't sue him like I would anyone else who would have done the same thing to me. What I did for him was a gift; I chose to walk away. There was no point in trying to reconcile that relationship. It's not going to help me in any way and it's not going to help him, either. I'll retrieve that money through other means, and although I was hoping to get a partnership in a very successful barbershop, unfortunately all I got was a screwing from my best friend.

Adrian taught me a lot. It's because of him I stopped arguing with people in a business context. When somebody believes they're right, there is no point in further discussion. If someone comes to me and wants to fight about something, I'll ask them, "How much do you think you got screwed for?" Then I'll write them a check and say, "Here's your money, now go away and please don't ever contact me again." Sometimes it's just easier to walk away from money. There is a cost to losing a relationship.

I don't want to sound completely cynical, because there are plenty of people you'll run across who want to help you and aren't out to con you or fuck you over. I met my friend Michele Morgan a little more than two-and-a-half years ago in what most people would describe as the oddest of circumstances. I was living in Los Angeles and late one night I was on Craigslist looking through ads and found a thrift store in Las Vegas that was seeking to liquidate. I arranged a trip to Vegas to inspect the inventory but had advised the seller I had to bring my dog Lucky with me as I couldn't leave him at home. This adventure posed challenges almost from the very beginning.

To start, a passing truck kicked up a rock, cracking my windshield. Lucky then became lethargic and unusually car sick. I called my appointment in Las Vegas to inform her I would be running a bit late.

"Will you be hungry?" she asked.

"A sandwich would be great, but please don't inconvenience yourself in any way." Four long hours later, we arrived in Vegas.

I walked into this giant thrift store and standing in front of me was a beautiful lady who had set up lunch for us on a makeshift table. That was Michele. Her hospitality extended to Lucky as well; she had put out water and treats to ensure his comfort. We broke bread and started to talk business. Except things did not go as planned.

Lucky began vomiting and bleeding from his hind quarters. I embarrassingly asked if we could reconvene another day, scooped up Lucky, and began the frantic search for the nearest vet's office. Five days in Vegas of morning-to-night vet visits ensued, with me returning to my hotel room each evening exhausted and scared about my dog's medical procedures. But I didn't have to go it alone.

Even though I was three hundred miles from home and alone in a strange city, Michele was there for me — bringing treats, meeting me at the hospital, sticking by my side doing whatever was necessary. On the rare occasions when she wasn't there in person, she texted and called, offering to be of any service she could. We never did end up doing the deal. But what we both got was worth far more. And Lucky recovered one hundred percent.

Meaningful friendships only come a handful of times in one's life. In a society where relationships are built on social media rather than face to face, I consider myself fortunate to have Michele in my life; she has been one of the greatest gifts God could give me. Michele is not only a true friend and confidant; she is my warm blanket on a cold winter's day.

It's always important to keep your eyes open when doing business with friends, just to make sure no one gets taken advantage of. That also goes for people who start off as business contacts but become friends. When you know someone who's like-minded and you choose to do business with them, it is not uncommon to build a friendship moving forward. These situations can be just as toxic or caustic as my conflict with Adrian, except the difference when starting as business partners is you become familiar with their business habits and acumen. Friendships are not often transactional. Deadlines are more lenient, debts are forgiven, favors are traded at convenience, and this can be a deadly brew in a new venture. If you choose to ignore this advice and believe you have pure magic with whomever you are going to pursue your dream with, make sure your foundation is constructed on the same principles. Have a blueprint, an outline or some other sort of mission statement to ensure you are both pursuing the exact same goals. Vision is very important for the success of all business. Do not go forward with an individual who does not initially and thoroughly understand these principles.

Like Michele, I have many friends I've done successful transactions with and we are still friends today. As with Adrian, I've had many friendships that unfortunately went off the rails. True friends and honest business associates will always come along;

however, if you want to succeed, keep your eyes open and don't be conned. If someone's going to come out on the short end of a deal, don't let it be you.

Chapter 7

ALL IN

GO BIG OR GO HOME BECAUSE, AS THE GREAT WAYNE GRETZKY POINTED OUT, YOU MISS ONE HUNDRED percent of the shots you don't take. If you want to make real money, you have to risk real money. Unless you hit the lottery, you need to have money to make money; the more you have, the greater your returns are likely to be. You can't sit at home complaining about your financial struggles while simultaneously being unwilling to do anything or take a risk. No risk, no reward. But that doesn't mean you need to be reckless about it.

I know that gambling has little to do with entrepreneurship, business or a solid commitment to make reliable profits or money, but I live in Vegas. It's part of my daily life and it makes for a good analogy. I see people playing slots in the casino and the top prize on the machine is around five million dollars. These are progressive machines that keep increasing and you can only win the jackpot if you're playing five dollars a spin — not fifty cents. People will go in with a one-hundred-dollar budget and they will lose their hundred playing that fifty-cent button with a total upside of winning fifty, sixty or *maybe* eighty dollars. Not a chance at five million, which is life-changing money in anyone's book. You're going there to gamble, you're willing to invest a hundred dollars in the experience, why not step up and have a chance at the score of a lifetime? True, you're going to go through your money more quickly, you don't have the money to replenish your bankroll for the night, but you have an opportunity to at least win something big. Someone's eventually going to walk away with that money, why shouldn't it be you? Go big or go home or get out of the damn casino — and the business world.

As I quoted above, you miss one hundred percent of the shots you don't take. I've gone to warehouses where people complain, "I have so much inventory for sale but I'm not selling any of it."

"Well, where is it listed?" I'll ask.

"Nowhere," they'll say.

This is when I tell them, "No one is going to knock on your door and say, 'Do you happen to have such and such in your warehouse?' Get it out there. Because if you don't, you have zero chance of selling it. Zero. Take a chance. Spend ten dollars to make a hundred." Earlier in the book I also noted I took fifteen hundred dollars, used half on a warehouse and the remaining $750 on merchandise to flip online. You can make a tremendous amount of money with very little momentum. It's how you use it that takes the cake.

If you want to make real money, you have to be willing to part with real money. One of the biggest reasons I'm successful is I can lose a hundred thousand dollars and sleep as well as if I had made a hundred thousand. I am completely emotionless about the value of money, which gives me the power to take risks that will empower me to earn money. My ability to take risks is where I think I really excel, and there's no reason you can't learn that too.

When I was twenty-nine, I was finishing up the process of buying an apartment building in Canada with twelve units, except this deal was taking longer to close than I expected. I had $115,000 in my bank account as a designated deposit for the purchase and the money was just sitting there. I grew impatient with how long it was taking to close, so I began doing some research for a way to make more money in between — something I would not recommend for everyone. But again, your ability to risk is the only thing that separates you from everyone else. I found two truckloads of gear that Bauer, a top-end hockey company, was trying to liquidate. I spent $114,750, which at the time was the biggest liquidation deal I'd ever bought in my life. I had so much hockey equipment, I was swimming in it. Even though hockey season was just starting in Montreal, I lived in a hockey-crazed country and Bauer is a quality brand. I had to figure out how to dump all this gear fast, before my transaction was due for the building. It got to a point where the transaction was ready and I still had not dumped enough hockey equipment to close. I didn't have the money to complete it and the owner of the building was now threatening to sue if I didn't close by month end.

They said, "If you don't close on the first, we're keeping the deposit and we're coming after you for every penny we can."

I'd taken a big risk, but I knew that was the only way to get a big reward. I went all in. I said, "To hell with it, I'm going to take a quick gamble." I almost lost everything — but I didn't. I finally dumped the deal to a guy in Toronto and ended up making a thirty-thousand-dollar profit.

I walked away a winner simply because I was willing to fully commit myself, use all the assets I had at my disposal and take a shot. One of the most important qualities leading to my success has been my ability to take a risk. I've lost a lot of money in my life. I'm still able to go to sleep and say, "That's okay, I'll make it back, it's just money, just a way of keeping score." I'm able to ride the highs, survive the lows, get back up and invest again, and so can you. My ability to deal with risk has been my worst enemy and my best friend; risk has made me a fortune and lost me a fortune and I'm still in the game taking chances. All in.

I'm sort of like a gambling addict, only I'm an addict investor. An addict businessman. I'm an addict entrepreneur and going all in is a huge part of that. I want to win it all and am willing to risk walking away empty-handed in order to get the big score. If you think about the greatest success stories — Ford, Kroc, Gates, Jobs — they were all people who were bold, took huge chances, and weren't satisfied with the meager triumphs most people are happy with day to day. They knew they might come up short, but they also knew without going all in they wouldn't reach the top of the mountain.

The chronic entrepreneur addiction is something that when it's in you, it's in you. Many people have it, but they don't know how to manage it or how to properly use it. A lot of people think they can learn how to succeed by going to business school. You're not going to learn how to run a business from business school. You're going to learn theory. You're going to learn examples. You're going to learn rules and principles, but you will not learn how to be an entrepreneur. Some of those concepts might be valuable to you, and if they are, buy and read the curriculum textbook. Watch YouTube; why spend fifty thousand dollars on theory when you can accomplish an equivalent with two weeks and forty hours of reading time? This is not a tirade to abandon college, but there are faster and more efficient options. Life experience, trial and error, that's what's going to really turn you into a winner. Either the passion is in you or it isn't, and if you're like me you eat, sleep and drink business twenty-four hours a day. It is said that ten thousand hours are required to become a master of anything. Do you want to master the business world? Invest ten thousand hours. Of course, you are going to fail, and among these failures you will find profound successes, but if you go all in, your first one hundred or one thousand hours will be life changing. You will become an addict of success.

The point of this book is to share all the risks I've taken, to take all my failures and all my successes and inspire people like you. Inspire you not to give up. Remind you that tomorrow is a chance to start over, that everything happens for a reason (even if you don't understand it at the time) and when you look back at your life you will be able to connect the dots.

When you go all in, sometimes you win and sometimes you lose. Although it would be nice to come out a winner on every deal, your goal is to win more than you lose in the big picture. You can't let momentary setbacks get you down, because that will reduce your willingness to take a chance. Fear makes us cautious. And cautious people rarely make serious money.

On a philosophical note, going all in can apply to many facets of life. Along with a majority of the topics I have covered, going all in can sometimes be life changing. When I was twenty-one, I saw a movie describing a coming-out story about two guys. It really affected me. Although I'd had girlfriends, I woke up the next morning and said I'm not going to live a lie anymore. I liked guys, always had, and it was time to take the risk — go all in on that fact and let the chips fall where they may. I called my mother who was working at the bank and asked her to lunch. She knew it was important because I never asked to see her in the middle of the day.

By the time she arrived to meet me, I was shaking and crying. She asked me what was wrong and I said, "I can't tell you."

"Is it a health problem?"

"No."

"Did you kill somebody?"

Once again, I said, "No."

"Are you in trouble with the police?"

I shook my head.

"Well then," she said, "nothing else matters. Stop crying, it really can't be that serious."

And she was right. I told her I was gay and she said, "I've always known. Don't be ashamed of it." We went on, talked about it some more and it ended up being a very beautiful day for us.

The concept that there are worse things to cry about has stayed in my head ever since. Every time something bad happens or it looks like I'm going to lose, I'll always ask myself, "Did I kill somebody? Am I going to jail? Am I dying?" If the answers are no, then there are truly always worse things to cry about.

Did you lose money? You'll make it back. That particular deal might not have worked out in your favor, but at least you took the risk. At least you had the balls to do what most people would never have done in the first place. And you learned from it.

When I leave the casino and I lose, I say, "You know what? You're perfectly happy to take their money when you win, so have the balls to let it go when you lose. Tomorrow's always another day."

Go all in. Be bold. Be smart, but be willing to step outside your comfort zone and risk. That's what the big winners do.

Chapter 8

REFUSE, REBOUND, RELOAD

REFUSAL IS A STATE OF MIND:

- Refuse to let them beat you down
- Refuse to give in
- Refuse to fall off the horse and not get back on

Resilience is the opposite side of this coin. Practice resilience in everything you do. If you've lost everything, if you're flat on the ground with nothing but the clothes on your back — use that to rebuild and reload. I know it's easier to say than do, but if you sit back and do nothing, your situation won't improve. It will only get worse. Realize you're still in the game and you've got nothing to lose. That's a powerful realization and one that gives you the upper hand in dealing with people who are playing it safe and trying to protect what they have rather than taking the risks necessary to truly achieve success. Necessity is the greatest building block of success and innovation.

I have a very realistic view of how the world works. I understand how small we are and how most things people put importance on is of very little consequence to life itself. I also understand the only limitations you possess are the ones you create for yourself. Reading this, what do you think about that concept? Despite even mental or physical setbacks, in the big picture you are entirely responsible for how you see yourself and how you behave. Why make things harder and believe even for a second you cannot do something? You're all you've got, so use it.

I often look at people working a regular job, earning ten or twelve dollars an hour, and I wonder how they are able to get up every day, go into work for an eight-hour shift, make eighty dollars before taxes and not be encouraged to try anything else. I can think of a hundred ways to make more than eighty dollars a day, every day, and be working to build my own dream instead of that of someone else. But yet people work week in and week out struggling to keep it all together. I understand that some people are made to work and others are made to fly. If you are reading this book, it's because you want change, you require more than a regular nine-to-five. So the real question is, what's stopping you from doing it?

Not every opportunity might be the right match for you, but if you find yourself refusing every opportunity that comes your way, then the problem is not the opportunities themselves but your mindset. So many times, I have offered individuals deals that were amazing, and most of the time, people would not take them. Not because they did not understand the deal, but because they talk themselves into believing good deals are impossible to find. Agreeing to make a deal keeps you in control and prevents you from letting the other party pull the strings. Once you have decided in your mind to go forward, the only thing left to do is negotiate a price and decide the best terms for your end to be as favorable as possible.

Refusal is also a key component of resilience. When I lose at the casino, I refuse to continue pouring good money in after bad. I accept my loss and look to rebound another time. I've seen people scream for their money back. That's not going to happen. Collect yourself, go home and figure out how to make that money back. Work harder until you're back to square one — or better. You've taken the loss. What are you going to do? You can't turn back time. You can toss and turn all night, you can lose all your hair, it's not going to change what's happened. The transaction is done. You're out on your ass, now get back up and do something about it. It's not how you fail that determines how successful you are. It's how you get back up from those failures and rebuild yourself.

One thing that is crucial is to *never* set yourself up for failure. Why do most startups fail? They don't have the right budget and fallback cash for what they're trying to create. You also need to have enough money to see you through until people discover you. If you don't have the cushion to get you to the first sale and then to an ongoing, regular cash flow, it's going to be very difficult to sustain the business to the point where it becomes successful and starts pouring money into your pocket instead of the other way around.

Another huge factor is expectations versus reality. Many people get depressed when things don't take off the way they've imagined and they don't become an overnight success. Every "overnight success" I've ever been associated with came after months if not years of lean times as they built momentum. You must realize that in order to succeed you must start somewhere, and more than likely your business is going to slowly creep up just like a stock gains value in the market.

Everybody thinks that I buy something for five dollars and sell it for a million dollars or that I have some magic way of buying a stock for a buck and making a million dollars off it. It doesn't work that way. You have to possess a firm grip on fantasy vs. reality. Having a realistic view of what you're doing and a realistic perspective on the time it's going to take to get where you want to go is as important as setting realistic goals for yourself. It's not realistic to think you go from making a hundred dollars to earning a million dollars — but you can set a goal that says, "I made one hundred dollars this month, next month I want to make three hundred dollars, and the month after that I want to make a thousand dollars." There will always be ups and downs. Make sure you're working hard, your plan is solid, and you're transforming yourself as the market dictates. If you expect to become instantly wealthy or successful, it's definitely time to manage your expectations — you want to be a long-term success, not a flash in the pan.

The third reason most startups fail is lack of experience. If you're going into something you have no knowledge of, then a) you're an idiot, and b) your growth period is going to be longer than someone who has a lot of expertise. If you worked for a glass company for fifteen years and you leave to start your own business in that field, you're going to kick the ass of somebody who's starting from scratch and knows zero. If you're interested in starting a business in a field you know jack shit about, go get a job working for someone else and earn while you learn. You may only have to stay there a few months, but you'll get a chance to see the stupid crap they're doing along with the things that are making them a success, all on their dime, at no cost to you. I've always known I can learn ten times more from a business that's run poorly than I can from one that's killing it.

My final point on this, and the one I think is the most important, is if you want your startup to succeed, you have to be dedicated. I wake up every single day at 6 a.m., and by 6:25 my computer is open and ready to trade the second the East Coast market opens at 9:30 a.m. I am dedicated to sitting in front of that computer until the 1 p.m. closing. When the market closes, I start doing my own businesses' mail, shipping and billing between 1 and 3 p.m., and then it's on to something else. I keep going and going until 10 at night when I finally sit down on my bed — and start researching investments for the next day. I'm asleep by midnight. Rinse. Repeat. Five days a week.

On the weekends I'm shooting YouTube videos for my business, I do promos, whatever else I need to get ahead and stay there. If you don't eat, sleep and drink business, if you don't eat, sleep and drink your project, if you don't eat, sleep and drink entrepreneurship, if you aren't thinking about this 24/7, then it's going to be a hard climb up the mountain. Dedication is what gets you through the bad times and keeps you in the game until the big paydays start to hit.

Many times, I've held a check for one hundred thousand dollars like it's a hundred and the next day I've had absolutely nothing left of that money. If my life was on a different path, I'd be sitting on one hundred million in the bank with no worries in the world. But that wasn't my destiny. If you fail, use what you've learned from the experience. All you need to do is get up one more time than you've been knocked down.

Chapter 9

DON'T GIVE UP, FUCK YOU

I'VE BEEN DOWN IN THE HOLE. I'VE BEEN DOWN IN THE GUTTER. I'VE LOST IT ALL — AND I'VE REBUILT IT ALL. Every person who reads this book is going to take something different from it. What's important is you learning to take what life has given you and instead of just talking about what you're going to do, go out there and fucking do it. You can say what you want about how I did things, or how you would have done them differently. And, of course, being an outsider looking in, it's always easy to judge, but at least I was proactive in my journey and didn't give up. And I challenge you to do it better. I have always said I would rather work for myself and make ten dollars an hour than work for someone else making twelve. Don't say you're going to start next week. Get busy right now, this very minute. Go to work. Reach your goals. Take your ideas and turn them into reality. Excuses are easy to come by, you'll have one today, you'll have one tomorrow, you'll have one next week. Fuck you. You've had some bad breaks and things haven't gone your way? I get it. Go home, cry for a minute, get up, and climb on that fucking horse.

As I've written previously, I left Canada $2.5 million in debt and I could have walked away from it. I didn't have to pay most of it back. I wasn't planning on returning to my home country, I could have kept that money and bettered my life in the United States. That same week, the person I was dating at the time left me. And it was also the week I lost my American Express Black Card, the one pinnacle I worked so hard to get and knew I might never see again. I was getting calls from Porsche that they were going to repossess my car for nonpayment. My entire world was crashing down. My parents weren't really talking to me, at least temporarily. They were angry at some of the choices I'd made and the situation I'd gotten myself into. I was really alone and lost and the only calls I received were from friends I owed money to, lawyers, and debtors. I remember sitting on the 30th floor in Aventura, at my friend Miki's condo in Miami, looking out at the ocean and thinking, *maybe I should just jump.* I was all alone; he'd gone back to Canada. As I sat there, I looked at my life and I said to myself, "What a fucking mess. How did I get here and where am I going to go from here?" If I was honest with myself, I knew how I got to that point. But it did little good to dwell on the past.

Most people would have filed for bankruptcy and that's probably what I should have done. It would have alleviated ninety percent of my problems, but there was a certain loss of pride about going bankrupt and I just didn't want to let myself go there. It was there and then I decided I was not going to give up. I was going to ignore all these calls while I rebuilt and then I would pay them all off no matter what I owed, down to the last penny.

There was one thing that was completely out of my control, which turned out to be an asset. My credit was already ruined, so if I took a year to pay them back, if I took two years, my credit score couldn't be any lower; it had already fallen from 850 to 475, which basically means you're breathing and not much more. I couldn't fix that, at least not immediately, but what I could fix was making sure I eventually paid back everything. I made a list of every debt I owed. I decided to attack the smallest debts first and then build my way up to the biggest. I started with personal loans, because you don't want to owe a friend money. It's much easier to owe a company money than having a friend call and say, "Hey, where's my money?"

I committed myself to the plan. I closed my Canadian cellphone and opened a U.S. cell account and I just attacked and attacked and attacked. Every time I would get beaten down and told no or tried to make a sale that didn't work, I just kept going back again and again and again. Every time I made money — it could have been $275 — I'd go down my list and find who I could pay back. I'd call and say, "Can I pay you back your $275 please?" More often than not they couldn't believe I was calling to pay back such a small amount and I'd just say, "I'd like to get you paid, I owe it to you." I'd buy ten dollars' worth of groceries and knew that if

I just ate sandwiches, I'd save enough to pay somebody back and I'd sleep ten times better that night.

Over time, I paid off the $2.5 million in debt, along with probably another two hundred thousand to friends I owed money to. I paid off every penny. Nobody ever lost one dollar on me. As I've shared, when I called American Express to make the last payment of $125,000, I asked my representative on the line if they thought they were ever going to get paid. He said, "Since the first day I talked to you, I knew we would get our money, it was just a question of time. With the score you had and that much credit, something had to go very wrong for you. With that kind of credit rating, you're used to paying your stuff. You just needed time to put things back together."

I had the choice; I could've taken the easy way out. Hell, I could've decided to jump off that balcony and put an end to it all. But I didn't. I'm a regular guy, and if I can do it so can you.

Let's say you've read this whole book and feel like you have a decent idea on what being an entrepreneur is all about, or you think you understand what it takes to run a business. Let's pretend for a moment you have it all figured out.

Being a business owner and entrepreneur is stressful. I know I have illustrated nearly a dozen instances in my life where I have been screwed over or had stress levels many individuals cannot imagine. The purpose of this book has been to inform you of the incredible toil awaiting you on this path. I am going to share a couple more memories of moments I believe embody the true essence of entrepreneurship.

My father is an incredible businessman in his own right. Like myself, he has owned several companies in his lifetime; he has also always been a shining example of what life is all about. I can remember a time he owned a hotel and on nights when a customer would check out early, he would go to the hotel himself, clean the room and bathroom, then attempt to book the room to someone else so as to not lose out on potential revenue. As an owner, you don't have the luxury of taking time off. Exactly the same way I abandoned my four-day vacation to ship three items, you too will need to make seemingly disproportionate sacrifices. My father had a choice of going home that night and reading a book, or relaxing, and chose instead to make a few extra dollars.

There is a very clear and defined line between an owner and employee. When I owned a cafe several years ago, it was my job to do everything. I cooked, I waited on tables, I cleaned shit off toilet seats if it had to be done; I was the plumber too if need be. When you make the transition to work for yourself, there is a paradigm shift that must take place or you will not survive. You must realize you are only going to get paid if you choose to work. There are no paychecks if you don't work, you only get benefits if you give yourself benefits. I have unloaded and loaded trucks by myself because I was short staffed or the employees who were off for the day were unavailable to come in. Think about a time you held a minimum-wage job. At every job there are stellar employees who go above and beyond; they are a special breed. Think closer about the slackers, and excuse-makers, the unreliable staff who are lackadaisical and show up late. These are the kinds of people you will encounter as an employer and you'll often need to pick up the slack as a result.

Owning a business is a pain in the ass sometimes. You've got to love what you hate, but sometimes it is literally a pain. There was a time where I purchased 350,000 units of bedsheets from Disney and they decided to case pack them by three per box. The container was delivered at 8 a.m. with a six-hour window to unload 117,000 boxes by hand. I had two employees available and picked up another four in front of Home Depot. In the first four hours, four men quit because they couldn't handle the labor-intensive job. I had to split the remainder of the work between myself and the two men still standing. We had to finish unloading what should have been another four hours' worth of work between seven people in two hours with two already tired employees and myself. If I failed to have the shipping container empty and ready for pick up by the deadline, I would be assessed a hefty fine, and this would cut directly into my profits. Plus, I had no way to secure the container overnight so it had to get done. There was no choice. As an owner you must do dirty work such as cleaning toilets or moving 117,000 boxes by hand; it's all part of the cards you're dealt.

Remember that all of this work is sweat equity into your business. Remember and trust that it takes a year or two for many startups to really get going. All of the effort you are putting into your venture is worth something. My efforts on the sidelines have earned me tens of millions in my lifetime. My commitment to work ethic has not only taught me many valuable lessons on the art of entrepreneurship, but it has allowed me to excel in situations that make others crumble.

You want to kill yourself; you want to jump? Fuck you, you're not doing it, get back to work. Take your losses, get off the deck, pay what you owe and move forward.

Bad times end. You just need to be tougher than they are.

EPILOGUE

So where am I today? I currently live in my Las Vegas estate with my faithful Sheltie, Lucky. I am also fortunate enough to live close to many trusted friends and acquaintances. The purpose of this book is not to brag about my accomplishments, or how big and fancy X, Y or Z is. I am humbled by the experiences presented in this book, and your difficult times should help you reflect similarly.

By now you know I'm always *on the lookout* for the next big opportunity and I already have my eyes on a couple of very exciting enterprises in Arizona and California. If you'd like me to keep you posted, drop me a line at anthonyryan@arttonline.com and I'll add you to my personal mailing list. By the way, the "artt" in my email address and the cover of my book stands for Anthony Ryan Transforms Tomorrow. That phrase, which I've included several times throughout this book, is my mantra. It's the guiding principle of my life.

I continue to run my successful online business organizations 24/7, and *I love what I hate* more than ever. I encourage you to go out and find what you love and find something you hate. There's a good chance you can make them work together.

POSTSCRIPT

THANK YOU FOR ACCOMPANYING ME ON MY ENTREPRE-NEURIAL ADVENTURE! IT IS MY SINCERE HOPE THAT YOU have found one or more of the concepts, stories or lessons in this book to be helpful as you navigate the ups and downs and highs and lows of this unique life we have chosen for ourselves.

As you know by now there are plenty of easier, and "safer," paths you could follow. Except, none are more exhilarating — or personally satisfying — than building your success from the ground up and being able to confidently look at yourself in the mirror and say, "I've made it."

As a fellow entrepreneur, please know that I have the utmost respect for you, your work ethic, and your business acumen as you fight the good fight every day in your pursuit of Transforming Tomorrow. You are the building blocks of America. You're thinking bigger, better, and inventing new ways to impact the world around you. I applaud all inventors; I salute the single parents following their dreams; and I graciously extend gratitude to the parents, role models, and mentors of today's and tomorrow's youth. Of course, there are those of you reading this book who do not have these positive influencers in your lives. You bravely persevere every day. Go out there and show the world what you're made of; fuck the naysayers.

My story doesn't end here. (And neither does yours.) If you'd like to continue to follow me on my journey, please visit my latest venture at www.arttonline.com. You can also check in from time to time to @arttonline on Instagram or search for my channel on YouTube.

If you have any feedback on this book, constructive or otherwise, or want to share your own story, please feel free to contact me at anthonyryan@arttonline.com. I would love to hear from you.

Thank you again. It's your move. Will you fold or go all in?

ABOUT THE AUTHOR

Entrepreneur, innovator, author, influencer —
Anthony Ryan Sadana has enjoyed a multi-faceted,
successful career in a wide range of businesses. He's
run retail operations, consults for both large and
small companies, has his own real-estate investment

organization, and is involved in a series of highly profitable online ventures.

Now it's your turn to put his hard-won knowledge and insights to work as you create your own success story. Anthony Ryan will be rooting for you.